YOU CAN TELL THE WORLD

Sherwood Eliot Wirt
with Ruth McKinney

New Directions for
Christian Writers

AUGSBURG PUBLISHING HOUSE
MINNEAPOLIS, MINNESOTA

YOU CAN TELL THE WORLD

Library of Congress Catalog Card No. 75-2834

International Standard Book No. 0-8066-1479-X

Manufactured in the United States of America

CONTENTS

Introduction 5

1. Writing Great Christian Literature 11

2. Direction Signs 23

3. Put in the Sparkle 35

4. Writing Is a Craft 45

5. The Significance of Words 55

6. The Effective Use of Words 67

7. The Light Touch 77

8. The Strong Touch 87

9. To Market, to Market 99

10. The Way of a Manuscript 109

11. Recycling Your Article 117

INTRODUCTION

Christian writers today face the most favorable opportunity offered them since the invention of printing. Each week a million new persons are learning how to read. Every few days a new Christian bookstore opens. The demand for Christian writing of quality far exceeds the supply. Meanwhile the human race is experiencing a depletion of worthwhile literature; people are famished for righteousness in print. Millions of men, women, and young people long for good words, helpful and hopeful words, relevant words, Spirit-filled words of strength and assurance.

Where are the trained professional writers who will set forth the truth about good and evil in the idiom of our time? I believe they are everywhere. The purpose of this book is to find them, encourage them, and set them to work.

Because I spent a quarter of a century trying unsuccessfully to break into print, I have a particular interest in bridging the gulf between writers and editors. I now see that from a human standpoint, my long dry spell was quite unnecessary. The simple expedient of seeking advice from the right people can make all the difference to an aspiring writer. Therein lay part of my problem: I was not ready to seek advice, let alone heed it.

For the writer who is prepared to submit himself to the rules, there is no limit to his outreach, influence, and effectiveness in the spreading of God's Word through literature. God never neglects an available servant. I believe that Christian writers should be moving into positions of spiritual, intellectual, and cultural leadership in the world. They should become chaplains to the reading public. They should infiltrate the whole field of modern communications, providing a Christian understanding and analysis of people and events.

Writing is only a means to an end. My deepest concern is not for the writer but for the person who reads. What people read, they become. It is not well known, but it is a fact, that every great movement to sweep through the human race has been brought about through writing. That the pen is mightier than the sword is not rhetoric; it is history.

Think of the reformation of Israel that took place under Josiah as the result of Hilkiah's discovery of a book in the temple. Think of Christianity itself, carried on the wings of Holy Scripture across the ancient world. The echo of Apollos' sermons long since died out in the hills of Asia Minor; we have no knowledge of the preaching of Philip that brought such great joy to Samaria; yet the sermons of Stephen, and Peter, and Paul have inspired the church for two thousand years, and if the Lord tarries, will do so for generations to come. Someone put them in writing!

The Reformation of the sixteenth century was first of all a literary activity. John Froben published Martin Luther's tracts in Wittenberg and circulated them all over Europe. Zwingli read them in Switzerland, Calvin in France, Cranmer in Britain, Ochino in Italy, Valdes in Spain, and the Reformation was under way.

Modern-day Communism did not capture two-fifths of the earth's surface through tanks and missiles, but through the writings of Karl Marx, a journalist. Maoism took control of China not through the actions of the "red guards," but by the mass distribution of the "little red book."

A minister at one of our Schools said to me, "Every Sunday I preach to about 100 people in my congregation. But every day I reach 3000 people through my column in our daily newspaper."

Today's reader is exposed to an unprecedented clamor for his attention. Yet the time comes when the right piece of literature, placed in his hands, can effectively transform his behavior and character. He will take it home, read it, reflect quietly on his own life and its meaning, and perhaps offer up a prayer to God.

That is what God wants and expects of Christian literature and of those who write it.

The thoughts that occupy these pages have developed during 15 years of occupying the editorial chair of *Decision* magazine. During that time a revolution has taken place in the writing business. All kinds of nonsense—not to speak of violence and lust—have been given space in our hitherto respected publications. It would seem that when the devil took the lid off Pandora's box he found a typewriter inside.

In one corner of the contemporary literary jungle may be located the Christian writer, the Christian editor, and the Christian publisher. They too are looking for a market, and thank

God there is one. Seven thousand—or million—readers have refused to bow the knee to Baal. While nonfiction continues to crumble into journalese, and fiction into moral anarchy, the human spirit still seeks fresh ways to express its relationship to its Creator. That expression is the writer's task and the reader's delight.

The sin of the race has never quite destroyed our memory of the Garden of Eden. The tree of life that stood in that garden, and which Adam never tasted, is available now in the Paradise of God, if we accept the words of Jesus in Revelation 2:7. It is the Christian writer's privilege, then, to spread a table of the fruit of life in the name of Christ, and to invite everyone who will to come.

I wish to express my personal thanks to Ruth McKinney, editorial secretary of *Decision* for the past twelve years, for her skill and enterprise in putting together these lectures that have been delivered over the past decade at various Schools of Christian Writing. I have edited them for publication, but the basic work, and the idea itself, have been hers. Mrs. McKinney is president of the Minnesota Christian Writers' Guild.

I would also acknowledge the friendly help of other members of the *Decision* editorial staff and of the editors of Augsburg Publishing House. To all of them I pass along the encomium of the Psalmist: "The Lord gave the word; great was the company of them that published it."

S.E.W.

1

WRITING GREAT CHRISTIAN LITERATURE

During the Vietnam War I watched a United States Marine Corps infantry training regiment in action at Camp Pendleton, California. These young men were at the end of three and a half months of boot camp training, and had been honed to a fine edge. Their physical conditioning was superb, but I was even more impressed by their mental conditioning. The Marines seemed convinced that the safety and future of the free world lay in their hands.

Here were young men posted on the ramparts of freedom with the strength and skill to turn back the enemy. They stood between democracy and the slave state, between the free man and the tyrant. And because they believed it, they crawled hour after hour through the mud; they acquired skill and knowledge in the mastery of their weapons; they learned to exercise restraint and control over their own lives; and they subjected themselves completely to those in authority over them.

I came back from that Camp Pendleton experience with the determination that I would stop playing around with my typewriter. Either we Christian writers mean business about winning souls for God, or we should go out of business. Either we believe that the gospel of Jesus Christ is the supernatural answer, a better answer than the Marines' firepower—in fact, the only answer—or we should be honest enough to retreat with our doubts and leave the field to someone who still has a mustard seed of faith.

If we believe God, and if we do have a sincere purpose and intent to serve him with our typewriters, then we will have to put first things first. In an age when everything from politics to television is demanding a priority on our attention, it will be tough. If you have been ordained to write, woe to you if you put everything else first. Woe to you if you do not give to God the best part of the day, when you are most alert, when the birds are singing and the juices are flowing and the mind is creative.

I believe that with motivation, with discipline, with good contacts and proper tools, Christian writers today can become effective voices for God. And they might even produce great literature.

What is great Christian literature? It is not necessarily brilliant prose, or significant poetry, or powerful drama, although it has been all three.

Great Christian literature is above all else that which carries the royal stamp, that which the Spirit of God has consented to use in the reshaping of human life. It is causal literature. It does things to people. I have deliberately added the adjective "great" to "Christian literature" because I am convinced that greatness rather than volume is the need of the hour. We don't need pious slush to replace ungodly slush.

There is a vacuum in the reading that is currently available for North Americans. A glimpse at the book stall at the airport will suffice to show the dearth. Alfred A. Knopf, a veteran publisher, says of the present crop, "Writers can't write—and when I say write, I'm speaking of a simple, clear, decent English. We allow ourselves to be manipulated. We've become a bunch of slobs."

What an opportunity for the Christian writer! Good people everywhere are revolting against the writers who traffic in obscurity and symbolism and sex. But no one, good or bad, will read your writing unless you have first been lifted out of the mind-set of ordinariness and conventionality, until you have graduated from the ranks of Sunday school prose and into the strong, clean, earthy temperament of the New Testament itself.

Great Christian literature, then, is what you will be writing in the months and years ahead, after you have been unshackled from insecure fears and personal conceit and bad habits of composition, and have become padlocked to your typewriter, your Bible, and your synonym finder.

Were I to list the literature which (apart from the Bible) has affected our age, it would include some of these titles:

Darwin's *Origin of Species,* Marx' and Engels' *Communist Manifesto* and Marx' *Das Kapital,* Kierkegaard's attacks on Hegel, Nietzsche's *Thus Spake Zarathustra,* Sinclair Lewis' *Main Street,* Hitler's *Mein Kampf,* Hemingway's *A Farewell to Arms,* Kafka's *The Trial,* Camus' *The Plague* and others.

These books, the most influential of our time, deal primarily with the scientific challenge and the loss of meaning in a mechanistic society. There has been no Christian work written since the novels of Dostoevsky that could honestly be said to match them in boldness, in documentation, in breadth and scope, in vision, in appeal to the human spirit, or in grasp of truth. C. S. Lewis is the only Christian entry in the field. The opportunities are wide open, and there is plenty of room at the top.

What then are the essentials of great Christian literature? What are the characteristics of the writing that we need to produce to enter the lists and compete for men's minds in the name of Christ? I will mention a few.

1. *Put the language to work.*

Billy Sunday once said, "If the English language gets in my way, so much the worse for the English language." You may laugh, but that is the proper attitude for a writer. Any editor can go over our stuff and delete the adverbs and correct the bloopers, but only we can write. We are not to serve the language, but to make the language serve us. Shake it by the scruff of the neck as a terrier shakes a rat.

Ah, but you say, "I haven't been to graduate school. I never studied Shakespeare." It is not a matter of education. Will Rogers wrote a daily newspaper column that appeared on page one all over America—it was enormously popular. I forget which college he attended!

When we really take hold of the English language and begin to swing it around, as a hammer-thrower swings his ball, you can be sure somebody is going to duck. We will be accused of manhandling the mother tongue. I wouldn't worry about it. As Mrs. Malaprop said of a critic, "Illiterate him, I say, quite from your memory." Suppose the language does become a fire hose in your hands, and the big words or the strange words are hard to control. Hang on! Some of the water will get where you want it to go.

A primary goal of the writer is to be published; and the chances of being published with a souped-up vocabulary are infinitely greater. Don't be satisfied with a vague twenty-five-cent word when you can have a crisp five-dollar one if you only take the trouble to open a synonym book. We don't need to take courses in vocabulary building. All we need is to stop reading the "funnies" and to start filling our minds with material that does some credit to God and our intelligence.

Summon the language, then, to your side every morning as you sit down to write. Treat it not as an object of worship but as a servant. Make it do your bidding. I will have more to say about the use of words in the chapters that follow.

2. *In great Christian literature all clichés have been guillotined from the text.*

Now there is nothing inherently wrong with a cliché. Its only fault is that it has been wrung dry. We can take any expression whatever, including the expression "accept Christ as your Savior," and use it so often that it becomes hollow and empty of connotation. That does not mean the expression is not good; it has just been worn out, and people will not listen to it—or to you—any more.

Webster defines a cliché as a trite phrase that has lost its precise meaning by iteration, a hackneyed or stereotyped expression. Now, what are some of the religious clichés that keep worming their way into our writing? I can think of a few: "he was gloriously saved"; "she went to the altar"; "he hit the sawdust trail"; "she was rescued from a life of sin";—or worse—"a life of shame"; "clasped in the arms of Jesus." Make up your own list.

But it is not only worn-out religious clichés that riddle our work. Think of such expressions as, "I can't get a word in edgewise"; or "due to circumstances beyond my control"; or "she kept a stiff upper lip"; or "this work keeps my nose to the grindstone." Our experiences are "salutary," our escapes are "hair-raising," our restraint is "admirable," our teeth are "pearly," our conclusions are "inescapable," our yells are "blood-curdling," our truth is "unvarnished." I repeat, there is nothing wrong with a cliché—the first time it is used! When these expressions made their appearance, they were great. But now our job is to step around them and mint some fresh ones. And notice that I said "mint" an expression, not "coin" it.

The problem of clichés, then, is not lack of vocabulary, or insufficient education, or mental block, or cultural lag. It is just laziness. We are too indolent to look for a better word.

3. *Great Christian writing has open windows.*

Editors become very sophisticated about manuscripts. They quickly scan the page to see if there is an illustration, and they read that first. If it is fresh and relevant and sparkles with a bit of humor, then our article is already two-thirds on the way to being accepted.

One good illustration can make writing live. In fact, illustrations often make the difference between readable Christian literature and routine pulp—and I can show you plenty of such pulp, ton after ton of it. I don't blame the denominations or the publishing houses. It's the writers! They are failing to make use of vivid illustrative material. *Crank out the next lesson, meet that deadline, throw in something godly, it doesn't matter whether everybody knows it already*—and wham! The presses begin to roll!

Most books of illustrations are of scant help.

I have been through many such volumes and find, on the average, one illustration per book that might be usable. That is a low batting average. On the other hand, a good dictionary of quotations or two is highly desirable. You might try *Living Quotations for Christians,* edited by Wirt & Beckstrom.

Then there is our own experience to be drawn upon. Personal illustrations are acceptable providing they are in good taste, are not too full of self-praise, nor too much given to detail, nor too self-revealing. We don't have to spell it out or spill it out; tell just enough so the reader will get the point. And when we have made our point, we should leave it. Let's not build a whole article on what our three-year-old granddaughter said to us. A drunk uses a lamppost not for illumination but for support. Let's not follow his example with our illustrations.

Another means of opening windows is the insertion of dialect. I commend the use of dialect and colloquialism as an asset to good writing. Shakespeare used dialect, and so did Dickens, and Lowell, and Shaw, and even Spurgeon. Yet all were masters of English literature.

Listen to this quotation from Dickens:

> "It's generally the worn-out, starving, houseless creeturs as rolls themselves in the

dark corners o' them lonesome places—poor creeturs as ain't up to the two-penny rope."

"And pray, Sam, what is the two-penny rope?" inquired Mr. Pickwick.

"The two-penny rope, sir," replied Mr. Weller, "is just a cheap lodgin'-house, where the beds is two pence a night."

"What do they call a bed a rope for?" said Mr. Pickwick.

"Bless your innocence, sir, that ain't it," replied Sam. "Wen the lady and gen'l'm'n as keeps the Hot-el first begun business they used to make the beds on the floor; but this wouldn't do at no price, 'cos instead o' taking a moderate twopenn-worth o' sleep, the lodgers used to lie there half the day. So now they has two ropes, 'bout six foot apart, and three from the floor, which goes right down the room and the beds are made of slips of coarse sacking, stretched across 'em."

"Well," said Mr. Pickwick.

"Well," said Mr. Weller, "the adwantage o' the plan's hobvious. At six o'clock every mornin' they lets go the ropes at one end and down falls all the lodgers. 'Consequence is that being thoroughly waked, they get up wery quietly and walk away!"

Now if we intend to use dialect as effectively

as that, one point is very important: it must be accurate. For example, if we plan to quote teenagers, it is best to discover for ourselves the way they really talk. Writing on the subject of youth will never approach greatness until we begin to reproduce their actual talk. The same goes for children. We should record not the way they talked when we were their age, but the way they converse together now.

4. *If you plan to write great Christian literature, go after the life.*

I said at the beginning that we are interested in causal writing, writing that does things to people, that forces them to a decision.

When we started publishing *Decision* magazine in 1960, our motives were earnest enough, but we didn't really know where we were going. Dr. John Bradbury of the now-defunct *Watchman-Examiner* had said to me that a hiatus existed in the current religious magazine offerings, and I was out to stand in that gap.

It did not take too many months of publishing to locate the target area. So now, when a manuscript circulates through our staff, we unconsciously ask of it a question: "Will this piece of writing help anybody?" And I challenge you, before you send another manuscript out, to ask, Suppose this is accepted, will it help anyone?

Will it toss a lifebuoy to someone in deep water? Can the reader identify with it or project himself into it? Will it give hope to someone living in quiet desperation? Will it touch on a person's real problem? Will it open the gates of the Kingdom of God to a sinner?

Whether it be a "How to" article or a "Why" article or a "When" article, or fiction—whatever it is—the bit of Christian writing should grapple with something significant in human experience and leave the reader a better person.

That, I may say, will not be done with sleazy composition. Let me be bold enough to propose some resolutions:

1. I will not write corn—banal, sentimental, obvious, stuffy tripe.

2. I will either seek to write imaginatively, or I will not write.

3. I will not waste my time on insignificant material.

4. I will write to change lives, if I can.

5. I will politely ignore those who would flatter me.

6. I will write in quantity but strive for quality.

7. I will thankfully give whatever glory comes to God, who alone imparts all gifts, including this gift.

2

DIRECTION SIGNS

In Christian literature, which is your business and mine, we have the greatest subject in all history, the Man from Nazareth. Beside this Man all the personalities on record from Abraham and Socrates to Mao Tse-tung appear in pastel shades. We have the greatest commodity, the gospel; the greatest book, the Bible; the greatest gift to offer, eternal salvation. If that doesn't motivate us to our typewriters, we're in trouble.

Our Lord had some interesting things to say to his disciples about ordinary people in positions such as ours. He said that if they played their roles well, they would be given more significant assignments. A Jewish girl named Esther, living in ancient Babylon, found that principle working in her own life at a most critical time in the history of her people.

What about today? What is God saying to us right here? I believe he is challenging Christian writers as never before. Such is the state of the world that the writing, publishing and distributing of books by God and about God may well mark the difference between divine mercy and divine judgment on our society.

I believe that writers will play a strategic part in the struggle for human hearts and minds during the next ten years. The people who run the computers, the scientists and engineers, the economists and industrialists and political leaders, as well as the "little people," are not machines; they need God. What shall we tell them about God? How do we describe heaven to an astronaut? These people want to know the truth about existence and its ultimate meaning. And I believe it will help us in our ministry if we can discern which way history is going; that is, if we can decipher and follow the new direction markers that have been posted along the trail of written communications.

The first marker that I see along the trail ahead in mass communication says *color.* The Christian literature of the future will be a great deal more colorful than it has been. That is all to the good. Nothing is more tedious than a dull religious book—I don't need to tell you that. Not even the poultry report of the Department of Agriculture can compare with some of the drivel that Christian readers have had to put up with.

Not only is there better art, more white space, more attractive page design, more illustrative material, better paper quality, more interesting and more readable type faces; but there is also a better writing style in Christian books. Gone already are the long, heavy-footed sentences; gone are "alas" and "alack" and similar clichés of eighteenth-century vintage. Good Christian writers today choose their adjectives judiciously and tend to forget the adverbs. They are learning all over again that the English language has marvelous flexibility. They are experimenting with words, giving the language its head, not hesitating to employ the colloquial or youthful jargon, to add a dash of humor, to spruce up and clip the prose and make it more exciting.

Such writing takes a venturesome spirit. We are looking for salty characters in the Christian devotional field like Oswald Chambers and C. T. Studd and A. W. Tozer. To a person considering the writing field I pass on what C. S. Lewis said to me: "Writing is scratching where you itch."

If you don't itch, why bother to scratch? But if you do itch, don't try to write a book unless you are fully prepared to let your own colorful self come through on the pages.

The second post I come to tells me that literature is becoming *more factual and realistic.* Tomorrow's religious book will be tightly written; it will tell the situation as it is; it will seek to reproduce succinctly on paper what people are seeing and hearing on their screens and already know to be the case. That does not mean that the Christian writer is doomed to reporting minutiae and irrelevant details. Far from it. Instead, when the Christian message is written, it will be set out in straightforward fashion, without bloomers or petticoats, without lofty phrases or purple passages, colorfully yet simply, in language that is chaste and that moves purposefully to its point.

A third post on the trail tells me that literature will spend *less time on detail.* Communication will be brief and on target. The whole story will not be told—"just the facts, ma'am." The author will try to get the big picture and some of the basics, but people will have to fill in the rest for themselves. People simply will not allow time for reading. It's their loss, but that's the way it is. We are trying to master techniques that will force people to take more time. We hope to write so appealingly that people will just give up and sigh and sit down and read the piece or the book. That means enormous emphasis must be placed on the opening, on the first and second paragraphs.

The fact that books are generally shorter does not mean that they will require less effort; on the contrary, they will demand more basic preparation and more discipline on the part of the writer. The author of the '70s who will really influence his day will be a person who knows the English language and the writers who have mastered it. Journalism courses are no substitute for a grasp of Geoffrey Chaucer, William Shakespeare, John Milton, John Bunyan, Jonathan Swift, Samuel Johnson, Robert Browning, or even Ernest Hemingway. To live in the twentieth century and to understand it, one must not only know these men; one must also know Søren Kierkegaard, Karl Marx, and Fyodor Dostoevsky. There is no easy way to master such men; if we haven't read them, sooner or later our bluff will be called. And may I add that I feel there is very little God can do with a lazy Christian writer.

The fourth signpost I would point to is marked *greater influence.* It is paradoxical that as the number of magazines and newspapers dwindles, their importance increases. Christian book publishers in America are breaking all records. They are selling more books than ever before. Christian literary giants are scarce in our day, but such as we do have, people are reading. This means that the opportunities are wide open for young writers. More than that, many authors are being snapped up by television.

TV commentators are now helping America to make up its mind. These journalists have become the national interpreters of our day. Television has not yet developed its own experts, its own schools, its own training programs. It is leaning on individual authors and journalists who can discern the signs of the times. They are being sought out and presented to millions of viewers. In the increasing chaos of our exploding society, think of the need for wisdom, for profundity, for depth of analysis! Think of the need for a Christian understanding of men and events, for a biblical point of view that nails sin for what it is and points to a solution that draws on all the resources of the universe!

The Christian author who speaks to the modern world will need to know not only his Shakespeare and his Marx but also his Augustine, his Luther, his Wesley, his Karl Barth, and his Carl Henry. He will need to be a disciplined person, and for his education he should choose, if he can, the finest, most biblically-centered seminary in the country.

When I speak of the increasing influence of the Christian author in today's world, I do not mean to establish an unfair comparison with other forms of communication. What difference does it make what medium God chooses, just so the seed is scattered on good ground? Are we so sick of mind and soul that we cannot say with Paul, "In every way Christ is proclaimed, in that I rejoice"? I praise God that he is using many media today, and using them mightily. If I am partial to the written language as an instrument of communication, it is because I have learned to appreciate its qualities of availability and permanence.

A man may take home a book, cloth or paperback, read it in a moment of quiet and be moved to reflect upon his life, when an oral proclamation will never penetrate his inner defenses. In such a setting, the prose must stand on its own merits. It cannot lean on an inflection in the voice or a pointing finger or a dramatic pause. Good writing is a cultural achievement. It probably stands higher in the scale of civilization than any other form of communication except the fine arts. It provides a magnificent medium for the transmission of ideas. The late Kenneth Strachan once told me that 85 percent of all Latin

Americans who have come to Christ have been won by a book, a tract, a pamphlet, or some form of evangelical literature.

Just what is good writing? It is not a calling, for God calls the whole man and not just his typewriter. It is not a trade or a profession, for very few men ply it successfully. It is not a hobby, for it absorbs more attention than any hobby should. It is not a gift, as a singing voice is a gift; in fact, few writers are truly gifted.

Good writing is a craft. It demands skill achieved through hours and years of toil and diligent application to the disciplines involved. A sculptor learns sculpturing by chipping marble, a woodcarver by wielding a knife. Just so, a writer learns to write by writing and rewriting, by cutting and polishing. Among the essential elements for mastery of the craft are powers of observation, objectivity and honesty, and a willingness to allow one's work to be improved. But perhaps the most important discipline for the aspiring author is to write something every day.

Whether a person is a topflight Christian author does not depend upon appearance, charm, skin color, bankbook, status, age, ancestry, or sex. It does depend, more than most of us realize, on willingness to consult the dictionary and synonym finder, to seek out friendly and dependable critics, and to rewrite his own material. And because writing is the most democratic of all crafts, the zealous Christian who feels ineffective before cameras and microphones can be greatly used of God through the written word to win thousands to the Savior.

A fifth signpost is *symbolism.* Christian literature seems to be on the edge of a revival of the use of symbols and images to express the truth of the gospel. Stage and cinema have been experimenting for years with types and symbols to express abstract ideas. In my city the Tyrone Guthrie Theater presented *Julius Caesar,* by Shakespeare; but Caesar was a modern South American revolutionary hero and Brutus was a capitalist and the upholder of the "establishment" who betrays the peasants in the name of freedom, while Antony was the confused liberal who is caught in between.

Almost three hundred years ago a classic allegory called *The Pilgrim's Progress* was outselling every book in the English language except the Bible. I feel safe in saying that the publishers of my modern version, *Passport to Life City,* would like to dock their lunar module in something like this; but I'm afraid they picked the wrong astronaut. Even so I believe a materialistic society is looking to the delightful world of story-telling for deeper insight into the truth that man does not live by bread alone. We shall continue to produce realistic literature, and even our allegories will be more realistic than they used to be. But the human imagination will not be confined to the gutter or the hog pen. C. S. Lewis' chronicles of Narnia, I believe, point us in a promising direction.

A sixth signpost that I see along the way to the future is marked *concern with real issues.* A good deal of ecclesiastical grapeshot has been discharged in the past in feuds among Christians. Great controversies have been raised over issues that turned out to be insignificant. David Lloyd George once said that he belonged to a church that had split over whether Christians were baptized "in" the name of the Father, Son, and Holy Ghost, or "into" the name. He said he felt strongly about his convictions in the matter, and was prepared to die for them, but he couldn't recall which side he was on!

Modern mass media will no longer permit Christians to be hung up on these issues. We are in a battle to the death, but it is a struggle over great issues involving the nature of the universe and the meaning and destiny of human life. Our controversies in the days ahead will be over primary, not secondary, matters; and if the particular social issue under discussion seems to be a tempest in a teapot, then it is up to Christians to place the whole in the perspective of eternity. H. G. Wells once lamented that all of his earlier books were pointless because he had built them around the current issues of the day which had since passed into obscurity. Let us not fall into that pit.

The times are new, the times are different. When Samuel Morse sent the first message over the Atlantic cable in 1844, the message read, "What hath God wrought!" When the first radio telephone communication between North and South America was established a few years ago, the first words transmitted over it were, "How's the beer down there?" When Sir Galahad took the field in quest of the Holy Grail he said, according to Tennyson, "My strength is as the strength of ten because my heart is pure." When Joe Namath took the field in the Superbowl he cracked, "There are four or five quarterbacks in the AFL better than Earl Morrall."

In such a sophisticated, cynical, disillusioned world, what can the Lord's scribe say that will connect with our generation? He can say that no matter how new and different our times are, they are still in God's hands. According to the latest confession of the Presbyterians, the key word for our day is "reconciliation." According to a "God is dead" theologian, Paul van Buren, the key word is "freedom." Radical militants tell us the key word is "justice" or "power" or "separate independence." But the Bible's key word is still "redemption from sin." Salvation in Jesus Christ is still the only message that can unkink the human tangle and lead men out of the swamps of hatred into the green pastures of love.

As I see the task of the Christian writer, it is to get this word of grace before the eyes of the literate world as colorfully, as coolly, as succinctly, as factually, as cleverly, as persuasively, as he knows how. And may God give the increase.

3

PUT IN THE SPARKLE

C. S. Lewis' autobiography *Surprised by Joy* is a beautiful work. He doesn't tell us very much about himself but just enough, and then we fill in the empty spaces in our own imagination.

The relationship between God and man is not a cliché, and God help us if we put it into the form of a cliché. It is not giving out a canned testimony filled with expressions taken from what other people said at a Bible-conference witness hour. Every day's testimony is fresh. Every Christian writer's witness should carry its own sparkle.

Let me now give you four characteristics that will add to your writing a sparkling quality. I have said that I avoid alliterations, and it's true, but these just happen to start with S: *smoothness, suspense, subtlety,* and *shock.*

Smoothness is what we continually try to achieve in *Decision* magazine. We devote precious moments to fussing about commas and semicolons. I once remarked to Billy Graham, "Do you have any idea how much loving attention is given to your sermons by our staff in the Minneapolis office?" Certain people have dedicated their lives to shaping the evangelist's material into something that millions of people will read and be blessed by. It is a marvelous ministry. And so we invert clauses, we transpose adjectives, we read over passages aloud to ourselves; and when we come to a point where we trip and stumble, we rework it and smooth it out.

Smoothness is a matter of practice, of muttering phrases to oneself, getting the rhythm and the alchemy of the language into one's head and heart and fingertips. We take hold of the English language and use it as a weapon. Don't let it overpower you. You are alive and the dictionary is dead. You can control the dictionary, you can control the language, you can make it say what you want it to say. Bend it to your purposes. You can even make up words.

The Bible's literary power lies not just in grandeur of expression but in smoothness. The

Authorized Version of Scripture was the work of 16th-century Englishmen, not one of whom was an outstanding writer. You probably cannot name a single person who translated the King James Bible, yet it is the acknowledged masterpiece of the English language, and as King George VI once said, it is the greatest gift that England ever made to America.

Suspense is the second point. Suspense draws a person into the next paragraph to find out what happened. It means we don't take all the marbles out of our pocket at the start of the game. We hold back the agates till the end. Now we don't have to manufacture suspense with a trick. It can be simply a skillful handling of material so we just don't give away everything in the opening paragraph.

One of the old rules of the storyteller was to say, "Now by the time I get through, you will see why he shouldn't have done that." Well, we can't be quite as open as that. We have to be more subtle than to say, "But I'm getting ahead of my story," yet that is the effect we seek to achieve. Just a hint to create expectation, to let people know that something unusual and remarkable will be divulged later in the article, something that might be just what the reader has been watching for. This is our goal. Our Lord Jesus Christ was a master of it, and so was the Apostle Paul in his famous plea in his own defense. All of these examples contain suspense.

The third point is *subtlety*. Subtlety is the gift of presenting truth in a way that overtakes the reader by surprise because he was not expecting truth, he was expecting something else. The subtle writer introduces his message in devious and interesting ways, by innuendo and inference and by nuance and by shading, and forces his reader to think through the implications and arrive at his own conclusion. This is a contrast to the slab-of-granite approach which is to be avoided in Christian literature. When we start a tract by asking, "Do you want to go to hell when you die?" we have lost our reader. Perhaps people did such things at one time when there was a dearth of literature, but they certainly don't do them today. The human mind will not be won by being overwhelmed. It will be won when it is challenged, when it is complimented, sometimes even when it is diverted.

There comes a point in our discourse when we talk about sin and salvation and we don't have to be subtle any more. There comes a time when we have to hit the reader over the head, and there is no need to be mealy-mouthed in presenting the way of salvation, the way into the Kingdom of God. Then we can call a spade a spade and a shovel a shovel; but we get there, not with a sandbag, but with a well-marshalled argument. We have been leading by a straightforward, simple, interesting, and subtle discourse into the very greatest issue of life, and we have not lost our unsaved reader along the way.

Read Paul's sermon to the Athenians in Acts 17. Scripture has only a capsule version of it, but he speaks of God being the God of all people, and then he brings his listeners to the hard fact of the resurrection. It's beautiful the way Paul adapts his message to different audiences. When he went to Corinth he preached Christ and him crucified, because Corinth had a different situation. Athens had an intellectual problem, Corinth had a moral problem.

Fourth, *shock*. The way I use it, shock means punch, it means vim, it means vibrancy, it means bounce, it means lift. Sometimes the only way a person can write with shock is when he is furious. There is plenty of shock in Paul's letter to the Galatians. He does not pay many compliments. He starts out, "You stupid Galatians." That is the text. "I am shocked," he says. "It is incredible what you have been doing."

Evangelistic writing without the quality of shock is apt to wither away into sentimentality or to evaporate into boredom. We have to punch out the gospel. We can take the reader along so long, and then it has to come through, otherwise we are not faithful to the gospel, and God help us if we are not. This is where the power comes in. We can write without this dynamic thrust and maybe people will print what we write, but that does not mean anyone will read it.

The hard-hitting words don't have to be violent words, just words of clarity. We can be kind, we can be winsome. Yet we will never capture the citadel of the human soul without this element of shock.

One could write a Christian novel and there would be only one line in it that spoke about Jesus Christ dying for our sins, and yet if it were put out in the airport in the bookstands and sold to the average reader, that one line could have more effect than a dozen books of unread sermons.

Sometimes I become disturbed about a subject, and I will sit down at the typewriter and righteous indignation pours out of me. Many scripts coming across my desk sound just like that. "Such and such a church is on its way to hell." We get that kind. Well, I sound off too; I am indignant, I am scornful, and I think I will just pulverize people with what I have written. Then I go to bed. Next day I read over that lush purple passage of prose, and I think, "What are you trying to do here? Why all this overwriting? You just threw away your argument. You had a case, but you ruined it by overstating it. You act as though God could not bring in the Kingdom without you sounding off. There is something insecure in your make-up."

So I just turn it upside down, and I rewrite it calmly and objectively. The indignation is still there, but it is rational, it is under control. We get our point across, and people will realize that we are saying something; we are arguing with alarm but are not going up in smoke.

Shock means a Sunday punch. Have you read *The Old Man and the Sea* by Hemingway? What is the moment of truth, what is the Sunday punch? It is when the first shark appears. The man has got the biggest tarpon that was ever caught in the Caribbean, and then the first shark hits the boat with the giant tarpon tied to it.

The Sunday punch in the story of the prodigal son is when the elder brother walks into the scene. I don't mean a trick ending. I mean a dramatic development, the unexpected introduction of something new, something that is a catalyst that changes the picture. This has been the hallmark of a good storyteller since the days of Aesop.

When I was a boy my scoutmaster was an immigrant from Australia; his name was Percy Shelley. He came from New South Wales, and he was one of the most wonderful men I ever met. He loved boys. He used to take us to Pirate's Cove in Marin County in California, and we would build a campfire and sit around the logs and look at the fire and we would say, "Shelley, tell us a story."

So he would tell us a ghost story, and we would sit listening. After I had been through such an experience once or twice, I was just half an inch off the edge of that log all the time because I knew there was going to come a point where Shelley would say, "And suddenly . . ." And my heart would just go boom like that. The Sunday punch. Shock us a little bit. That will make the story stand up and talk.

This really is the story of the human race, because Paul tells us while we were without strength, in due time, Christ died for the ungodly. While the world lay gripped in tyranny and wickedness, God intervened and sent his Son to die for us and to take away our sin. This is the Sunday punch. This is the story that you and I have been sent to tell. It is not a dogmatic formulation and it is not a preachment; it is a story. We are going to get further with our stories than with anything else. We are to write it in a new and compelling way, not to obtain personal fulfillment and self-realization, and not to justify our existence before God, but to help others to find Jesus as Savior and Lord

4

WRITING IS A CRAFT

I believe that if there are enough good writers and good publishing houses, people will buy books and read them. I believe that good Christian literature is always acceptable, outside the church as well as inside. Today the public is more receptive than ever to our product.

Editors are looking for people who are aware of the times in which they live, and who are not writing the way their mothers wrote; who are not turning out eighth-grade compositions, but who are writing in the modern vein. The editors want material that is alive, that pulses with a feeling that you know where you are—not in some ivory tower, but right downtown on the Mall. They want Christ in the marketplace.

The editors also want material that appeals to young people. Fifty percent of the population is 25 years and under. But we don't realize this, so we write for the dear folks at home, sitting in their swing in the garden, rocking back and forth and reading pleasant little devotionals. We need instead a youthful, zestful frame of mind.

The editors want copy also that has a fresh approach. A young man came to one of our writing schools, an athletic type, and I said to him, "Why don't you collect testimonies from famous athletes in America and publish them as a daily devotional?" A Christian house picked up the idea and published it. Now he has finished his second book and is working on his third.

How can we put our copy into marketable shape? How does the writer get his typewriter off the launching pad and his writing into orbit? I would list three stages for this rocket.

The first is, *make contact with the reader*. If we are going to make contact with today's reader, we cannot hide ourselves as our Victorian ancestors did behind the discreet hedge of semi-pious expressions and asides to the gentle reader, and all that sort of thing. There are no more gentle readers; they are all watching television. If a man does take the trouble to scan what you have written, do you know what he is going to be looking for? I know the modern reader; he will be looking for your angle. He will wonder, "Why is this person writing this thing? What's he up to?" The reader doesn't think that we really care about him. He wants to know, "What's this person's angle?" *Make contact and make a positive contact.*

Over thirty years ago I signed on as a quartermaster aboard an 80-foot Bureau of Fisheries vessel in the Gulf of Alaska. It was a convenient way for me to get from Valdez to Juneau across the Gulf of Alaska, a two-day trip, but it turned out to be the worst voyage of my life. We ran into a howling storm; it took us a week to get there, and when I got to the end of that journey I wrote the story and sent it to the Alaska *Sportsman,* a magazine published in Ketchikan, Alaska. The editor fired it back to me with this comment: "So you had a miserable time. Why inflict it on others?" Be careful in your writing that you don't take advantage of your facile pen to get rid of what is bothering you. Don't take your miseries and parade them in front of other people, trying to attract sympathy, trying to protect the image (that is what I was trying to do, so that the natural interest of the storm and the voyage was lost in the shower of tears).

The next stage is the *organizing of material.*

Three books in my filing cabinet never got off

the launching pad. One was written during my years in Alaska. It has a light easy narrative style, it has adventure, it has color, it makes contact with the reader. It was sent to many different publishers, and it bounced back. Finally, I arranged for a lady who had worked for Macmillan to read it for a ten-dollar fee. She told me: "This manuscript is not organized." I knew it, but I did not know what to do about it, and anyway I felt that stylistically it was such a gem that it did not really matter.

"Young man," said H. G. Wells to an aspiring young writer, "you have a style before you have a story, and God help you." I had the last interview with C. S. Lewis before he died. I asked him, "Will you tell young writers something about style?" He said, "Style? Say exactly what you mean, and when you have said it, be sure you have said exactly that. That is style."

You see, all I needed to sell my book to a publishing house was a structure, a skeleton, a table of contents, but I could not come up with it. I could not weave the narrative into the historical material so that the transitions were smooth. I had great globs of historical matter woven into a rowboat narrative, and it did not work. It will never be published, and it is a pity too because of all that cleverness!

Reduce everything to heads and subheads and 1, 2, 3. Get into the business of outlining, but don't let it show. The skeleton must never show any more than it does in our bodies. We clothe it with flesh, but the basic skeleton must be there.

Remember that sermon about a rich young ruler who came to Jesus? He came at the right moment, when he was at the right age, he came in the right mood, he came to the right person, he asked the right question, he got the right answer, and did the wrong thing. How is that for an outline? You go to church next Sunday and try outlining the sermon. You may end up changing churches!

A writer with average gifts can turn out a book, a good book, if he has a good outline, if his material is organized. A great help in organizing material is to ask, "What is the basic premise? What am I trying to say?"

Now a word about *transitions*. Transitions can be smooth or they can be rough. One of the worst transitions is a word such as "however" or "nevertheless" or "on the other hand." Avoid them. Try to make transitions undiscernible so that the copy moves logically from one point to the next.

Keep the progression simple! Go directly to your points 1, 2, 3, with a bright introduction.

The introduction, of course, is a separate thing. It should be lively, it should be catchy, it should be provocative—a grabber.

Then we move into our points and there must be no deviation or ellipsing. If you protest, "It is too simple and too short,"—well, after you have your structure you can drop in an illustration, something that a well-known person said or something that you have experienced, to illustrate the particular point being made.

A warning here about acrostics, acronyms, and alliterations. I know some of our most eminent churchmen use them, but I contend that while it may be cute, it is not literature. Five peas in a pod, or seven c's, or four d's, are unacceptable. You don't see them in Scripture. I know some ministers use them all the time, and they think they are fine. But by the time I have been led down the path of prayer, perception, purpose, perspicuity, perseverance, I am wondering if the next two points will be peanuts and popcorn. I don't want memory helpers, I just want the gospel. I want strong meat, not alphabet soup.

A third stage in getting our article published is *follow-through.* It is one thing to grind out a piece to fill a hole, to meet a particular need; but to do a saturation job, to research a piece, to pick up the loose ends, to check out the spelling, the documentation, the permissions, bring it up to date—these are the elements that bring a sense of completeness to the article and give it a flavor of authenticity.

You say you are not an authority on the subject? Yet one can always substantiate one's material. I am not an authority on sociology, yet I wrote a book on the evangelical social conscience. I documented everything and got by with it. It was criticized, but nobody said, "He does not know what he is talking about," because I listed my sources in the notes.

We don't have to be a living authority on a subject to write about it. Let us take an example: the ministry to the blind people of your state. Perhaps you are not the director of an institution for the blind, but you come in as an observer. You have your notebooks, you ask for the resources, you check out the literature, you get documentation. You can write the story. All you have to do is put the sentences together and have them make sense and follow the kind of outline that I have suggested.

The conclusion should relate back to the introduction and should in a subtle way summarize what has been said. And very important: make it end strongly. And then just cut it off. That is the end. We don't have to make a rehash or a recapitulation in the sense that "and so we see as a result that we must go ahead and decide this," or that sort of tiresome thing. Just cut it off.

Follow-through involves more than just tidying up the loose ends. It involves building through suspense to a climax. It involves holding back a key illustration with which to wind up the piece. It involves a satisfying conclusion.

I wrote my first book when I was 22 years old, on the shores of Hilo Bay in Hawaii, under the coco palms, in the winter of 1933 and 1934. It was an account of my 17 days as a deck boy in the U.S. Merchant Marine aboard the sugar freighter *Maunalai.* I was shepherding 44 crates of chickens across the middle of the Pacific, and the chickens got out, and they insisted on walking through the feed and tipping the water cans over into it, so that I had grass growing out in the middle of the Pacific. It was a funny manuscript, but it failed to sustain the tempo, and all of a sudden it ran out of steam. I had nothing more to say. I got myself to Hawaii and there I was, and I did not know how to cut it off or wrap it up. The literary agent said, "It is very entertaining, but it just is not going to make it." No follow-through.

We can help our subject by writing to very important people. I suggest we get as much material as we can on the subject. Build a big file. We will not use it all, but we can take a bit here and a bit there and piece it together. Get so much material you don't know what to do with it all. Sift it. Pick out the best illustrations and sew them into the article. Follow through and check out the material.

How many times have you read that while the *Titanic* was sinking the ship's orchestra played "Nearer My God to Thee"? Well, we researched it and we found that it was not the *Titanic* at all, it was the *Lusitania;* and it was not the orchestra, it was the Royal Welsh Male Chorus; and they did not play, they sang. But the tune was right.

Make contact with the reader, organize the material, and follow through to complete the job.

Since this is a chapter on craftsmanship, I would like to close it with a consideration of the writer's tools. No craftsman can do his best work unless his tools are sharp. Tools will not make a writer, but they will help him immeasurably.

I recommend an electric typewriter with clean keys and a fresh ribbon, plenty of good bond white paper, several translations of the Bible, at least two books of quotations, a good dictionary, a synonym finder, an atlas, subscriptions to magazines that reflect the writer's interest, and access to a standard encyclopedia. I would remind the writer that the public library has a reference desk that is always willing to help with research and even to send for books that are not at hand.

With such an array of material on his desk, and with the immediate needs of sleep, food, exercise, and sociability taken care of, the writer can then retire to his nook for three of the most wonderful hours of his life, working at his craft for the glory of God.

5

THE SIGNIFICANCE OF WORDS

Marshall McLuhan has announced that we have moved out of the age of Gutenburg into the age of television. The professor says that ours can no longer be considered a "linear era" but rather the era of symbolism and visual images. Unfortunately, he had to write a book to declare these astonishing developments and thereby ruined his point. The spoken word cannot eliminate the written word. Literature will be around as long as people are around; and when the last word is written, God will write it.

Without any doubt, words are among the most important things in the universe. When a person is unconscious, we listen first for the breathing, then we wait for the eyes to open, and we listen for the utterance, for speech, for words. Words mean life. "In the beginning was the Word." "Heaven and earth shall pass away," said Jesus, *"but not my words."*

Generals of the infantry will tell us that a good battle cry is worth many platoons in combat. But a battle cry is nothing more than a slogan, and a slogan is a popular combination of words: "Fifty-four forty or fight." "Hang the kaiser." "England, and Saint George." These are words, and by them people live and die.

Words are what distinguish man from lower forms of life. Observe a pet as it seeks to communicate with you. It will tell you why man is made in the image of God. As his Creator speaks, so man speaks. What a beautiful gift God has given us, this gift of language. I form words, you form them, and we hear and read each other's thoughts. We catch the meaning.

Then we turn on the television set and watch a street riot in Bombay between people whose chief point of enmity is that they speak different languages. This tragic sight tells us of the curse that befell man at the tower of Babel. People actually kill each other over words.

To us who are professional writers, words represent something quite different from basic communicability. As we know, every successful craftsman is familiar with his material. The building contractor knows his concrete formulas. The carpenter knows his grades of lumber, the tailor knows his fabric, the chef knows his grades of beef and his breads and vegetables. The miner knows his rock strata. The golf champion knows his clubs.

The writer is also a craftsman, and his basic material is words. His task is to arrange those words so that they express ideas that others will read and grasp. If he is successful, they will pay to read, and they will agree with what he writes. If the writer is an "idea man" as well as a "word man," he may influence a generation. People will hail him a genius. Most writers, however, are simply "word people." We draw our ideas from sources other than our own. We then couch them in our own words. For example, the Christian writer draws his ideas from the Bible, which is his best source. He does not claim originality; he knows the world will not be saved by innovation. Rather, he strives for interest and clarity.

The more we write, and the more use we make of words, the more familiar we become with them. We learn which words are clean and strong and which are second-grade lumber. We come to sense what arrangements of words will create a smooth effect, what will convey suspense, what will achieve subtlety, what will please, what will depress, what will sound the alarm, and what will simply titillate.

We have seen that words can kill. Words can also make alive. Words can make us wealthy, and words can involve us in million-dollar libel suits. Words can erode character and send people to hell. Words can also lead souls to the very gate of heaven.

Some words should be left in the dictionary. They should never be written, spoken, or even thought by a child of God. Other words should be on our lips every hour, and should appear in nearly everything we write.

To express oneself effectively, one does not need a large vocabulary. Abraham Lincoln did very well with a few well-chosen words. Many a writer's effectiveness can be said to be in inverse ratio to his working vocabulary; that is, the more words he uses, the worse his stuff reads. But at the same time I will never recommend writing "basic English." It is a shame to put limits on language. Properly used, a wide vocabulary can add great power to one's ideas.

Dr. Calvin Linton of George Washington University has declared, "One clear, well-constructed sentence is worth a thousand pictures." I have discovered that people are fascinated by words. Fifty percent of all genuine humor is made up of word play, and I don't mean puns. A punster belongs to the linguistic underworld. But a play on words is not only permissible, it is first class entertainment. We find such word play all through the New Testament, particularly in the letters of Paul. We find it in Jesus' encounters with the Pharisees.

In the Roman Empire a child's education was centered about words. If he could handle words, his success in life was assured. Rhetoric and grammar were the principal subjects of the curriculum, more important than mathematics, astronomy, geometry, or music. To turn a phrase well was more important than avoiding crime or immorality. There were fixed rules for composition; and if a Roman senator or a Greek orator were to listen to some of our legislators in Parliament or Congress, I think he would leave the chamber in disgust at the crudity of our speech.

There may well be a return to formal rhetoric in the years ahead. Meanwhile, in an era of unpolished verbalizing and illiterate culture, you and I have been handed the gift of language and have been told to use it. We will only turn out a fraction compared to the current pornographic and perverted literary output, but we hold the torch of truth. We are on the winning side.

Words are tools. They make us pros. You may not be a success, but if you can handle words, you will never starve; and you may become a voice for God in this generation such as you never imagined. What does it take? It takes work, effort, persistence, diligence, and discipline. You say, "I don't have a poetic imagination; I don't have the vocabulary; I don't have—" Just a moment. Do you have this book? *The Synonym Finder,* by Rodale? If you have it, you have all you need. Simply start to use it. That's what I mean by work.

The English language belongs to you. You don't belong to it. It is your servant, not your master. Language is a living thing, and it lives because you are using it.

We sometimes use the expression "murdering the English language," and it is a description of something very painful and very real. A colorful and colloquial use of language, of course, is always delightful provided you can understand what is being said. I may not always "get" the local color, but I enjoy it anyway. It sounds real.

Editors read manuscript after manuscript looking for interesting and exciting words and find so few. That is because most writers are lazy and won't look for a more interesting choice than the word that comes immediately to mind. It doesn't take much; we editors are pathetically grateful for any drops of color in your paragraphs. They must be appropriate; then cannot stick out too obviously; but they can do a lot for your writing. Originality and creativity do not mean discovering something new; there is nothing new under the sun. Creativity is putting old things together in a different and fresh way.

So it appears that if one is to speak of words, he must also speak of style, for style is the posture we adopt in our use of words. Style is personality expressing itself by putting words together in characteristic ways. Many writing styles have become popular in our day.

The one that comes easily to mind is that used by C. S. Lewis. It is *chatty and informal,* but never cheap. Lewis has succeeded in putting profound truths into everyday language, and making them seem deceptively simple. Our Lord Jesus Christ, of course, also exercised this gift. Such a style is easy to read and easy to understand, and is a great relief from the textbooks.

Another popular style is *reportorial,* and was introduced into literature by Ernest Hemingway. It involves a use of terse understatement, with heavy emphasis on technical knowledge. It seems to carry the ring of authenticity. Tell it the way it is, without editorial comment. Let the reader draw his own conclusions from the facts.

Another popular style, and I regret to say it seems to be increasingly popular, is *the prejudicial.* Many contemporary writers no longer are content to tell it as it is; they report on the basis of their prejudices and biases. They evaluate in terms of their own preconceived notions. For them the world is a stage, and they are reviewing the play—or to be precise, they are panning it.

Still another popular style is *whimsy.* Humorous writing is in great demand. Art Buchwald, Irma Bombeck, Jim Klobuchar are contemporaries; Robert Benchley, Dorothy Sayers, Will Rogers are earlier stylists of this type. Christian humorists would find a ready market today, but they are rare birds.

There are also unpopular writing styles, and unfortunately, they still have their proponents in religious circles.

One such style is *the hard-sell.* It is an evangelical favorite. I will not step on any toes, so I will say no more.

Then there is the *gee-whiz school.* It gives us excitement no end. We are breathless! So we stop reading.

Still another unpopular style is *the pious over-*

kill: sweet, sticky, cloying religious language, clichés galore, heart throbs of yesteryear. Unfortunately, some people still like it and pay to read it.

Now here are some ideas for you to consider in handling the words of a sentence. Notice I didn't say "Here are some tips," or, "Here are some suggestions." Why not? Because I don't want to convey that connotation. I am not giving tips; I am helping to circulate ideas. You are not my pupils; you are my fellow writers. It is a fine distinction but the right word will convey it. I had to go to the dictionary to find it.

1. Use active verbs instead of passive. Instead of saying, "Reginald was bitten by a snake," or "Reginald suffered a snake bite," or "Reggie was snake-bit," turn it around: "A snake bit Reginald."

2. Eliminate adverbs and unnecessary adjectives. To understand what I mean, read the short story that changed the whole tenor of North American literature. It was entitled "The Killers" and the author was Ernest Hemingway. I should say parenthetically here that adverbs and adjectives do have their place, as will be seen in a moment.

3. Avoid label words such as *conservative* and

fundamentalist. Avoid overworked color words such as "ghastly," "horrible," "beastly," and also "terrific," "smashing," "tremendous." My wife used to talk about city traffic giving her a heart attack, and now she has toned it down; she says she is having a cardiac arrest. Much more interesting.

4. Use the synonym finder when you are having trouble with a word and when you are not having trouble. It cannot fail to improve your material whenever you consult it. Examples: "asinine" to "foolish," "rejoiced" to "exulted."

5. Avoid using "I" too often in a testimony or in anything else.

6. Strive for understatement. In an age of superlatives, it is a technique that will not fail to attract attention if it is applied with humor. British humor is delightful because it is droll, straight-faced, and understated.

7. Avoid professional jargon as you would cyclamates in your soft drinks and phosphates in your washing powder. In American educational circles they use expressions like "in terms of," "frames of reference," "extrapolated," and "phased out." Watch for these traps. Some jargon is permissible; for example, you may get

away with the word "hangups" in an article—once. But the secret is to avoid repetition.

8. Don't play obvious games with words. Avoid conscious word play. Poe wrote, "The silken sad uncertain rustling of each purpose curtain." It was supposed to convey the wind blowing a curtain, but it didn't come off. Too obvious. Onomatopoeia must be treated very delicately.

I plead not for the elimination of adjectives but for their judicious and sparing use.

As for adverbs, here is an example of how they can be used in abundance with effectiveness:

> "May I seek to live this day quietly, easily,
> Leaning on your mighty strength trustfully, restfully,
> meeting others in the path peacefully, joyously,
> waiting for your will's unfolding patiently, serenely,
> facing what tomorrow brings confidently, courageously."

The chief reason our material is not being accepted as we wish it to be is not because our ideas are erroneous, not because our motivation is suspect, not because our illustrations are weak, or our logic faulty. It is simply because of what we do with words—words—words. When we clothe those words with flesh, they come and dwell among us, and gladden our existence. They may even by God's grace enable us to behold his glory. And if we cannot speak the unspeakable, what does it matter? God has already spoken; let him who has a typewriter put in a fresh ribbon.

6

THE EFFECTIVE USE OF WORDS

A few years ago I tried to find out which passage of Martin Luther's introduction to the *Letter to the Romans* it was that John Wesley was listening to when he felt his heart "strangely warmed." I went to the library of Augsburg College in Minneapolis and examined three translations, and they were all so different that I decided to tackle the original German. To my astonishment, the translations were only pale copies of the original; Luther's German I found to be rich, strong, earthy, and gripping, but the English equivalents were flat words, of Latin derivation, so that what came out of Luther in power ended up like the minutes of the Royal Botanical Society.

Had I to choose, I would much rather read

articles that used sharp, vibrant words in the wrong sense, than articles that used dull words in the right sense. Shakespeare was above all other things a master of words. Not that his vocabulary was so extensive, but he chose his words to convey vivid impressions. He was a word painter. So was Abraham Lincoln. And so can you be, if you take the trouble.

It is not a matter of genius, it is a matter of spending time. It is a matter of pausing five seconds before you write that key word, to see whether you cannot substitute a better one. When we are dealing with Anglo-Saxon derivatives, English can be a strong, almost brutal language, with tremendous expressiveness. This Teutonic element is what enraptured the Germans with Shakespeare; they look upon him as their own and claim the English don't understand him.

But I do not wish to decry the Norman and Latin elements in the English language, which add tremendously to its variety, beauty, and flexibility. One can say all manner of things in English that simply cannot be expressed in French or German. That is one reason that English is fast becoming the most popular language in Asia, after the native tongue.

To show what I mean by variety and expressiveness, I will ask you to play a game with me.

I want you to try to find a better word for the one I use. I want a word that is more specific, more colorful, more descriptive, more interesting. I will give you some examples:

A *bird* [chickadee] perched on the clothesline.

He drove up in a *car* [slightly battered Plymouth].

A *tree* [Ponderosa pine] stood in the yard.

The house had a *basement* [downstairs workshop].

A *sidewalk* [flagstones] led to the house.

He worked in *New York City* [Manhattan].

For a hobby he raised *chickens* [Leghorns].

There are so many things we can do with words if we spend time with them. Here are some suggestions:

Try not the first word that comes to mind, but the second. Instead of heathen, try pagan; instead of Jew, try Hebrew or Israelite or Israeli; instead of fundamentalist, try evangelical.

Pick up the jargon that people use around their work. Here is one of the best ways to add authenticity to writing. You will discover that the airlines refer not to their planes but to their equipment; the Coca Cola salesman refers not to his juice but to his merchandise; the baseball pitcher does not talk about his slowball and his curve, but about his change-up and his slider.

In the church there are also distinctions. Whom the Episcopalians call a priest, the Pentecostals call a minister, and the Lutherans a pastor. Baptists speak of parsonages, and ordinances; the Presbyterians of manses, and sacraments.

Get a nice feeling about words, an accurate, discriminatory feeling. Become friendly with words. New words can be tremendously exciting companions. Words are also great fun. People go into stitches over words. *My Fair Lady* was built on the way people use words. Dickens built his reputation in the *Pickwick Papers* on the way his characters manhandled ordinary words. If you would like to write about your own childhood, reproduce the exact expressions that your folks used—nothing phony, nothing corny, just the real article. Those expressions alone could sell your piece.

Now, having heard all this, you are faced with the immediate problem of writing an article. You know what you want to say, but you have a great fear that after you have put it all down with a great deal of effort, no one will be interested. But just for a moment come and sit behind the editor's desk and consider his dilemma. He has a magazine with a circulation problem. He cannot go out and hustle subscriptions to stay afloat. There is only one thing he can do, and that is to make his pages just as interesting and polished and sparkling as possible.

This may take a considerable amount of tinkering, but he is willing to do it if he has the time. He does not expect your manuscript to be perfect. He is willing to touch it up; but he does not want to rewrite it for you. If he edits a weekly, he may be forced to use your stuff as it is. And that is just what is wrong with so much of our evangelical literature.

I have in my files an article that is loaded with nuclear warheads. It is revolutionary in content, and it coins a new idea that is so arresting that the idea was picked up and made the basis for a lead article in the religion section of *Time* magazine. Yet the article is not well put together. It is prosaic and its lead is so dull that one wonders whether anyone under 50 would bother to read it. It begins by saying, "The purpose of this article is to suggest that each of the major Protestant denominations could wisely establish as an integral part of its theological educational system a new type of theological seminary."

Let's pause for a moment to examine this article. There is obviously more here than reporting or observing. A fresh idea is involved, something creative. So we begin to read, and we run into this lead sentence. The word "theological" is used twice. Worse yet, the author gives away the show. There is no suspense, no build-up. The page is flat reading anyway, without illustration. The author does say some things of great interest, if only we had the patience to pick our way over the rocky moraine of unpleasant, dull, heavy words.

Our task is to find new ways of stating scriptural truths, vividly, imaginatively, compellingly. We need a language breakthrough by a band of men and women writers who will give the world a 20th century Christian vocabulary that is as quick and powerful and sharp and piercing as that of the first-century church.

Consider how effective individual words can be in our titles. Here are three secular titles that arrested the attention of the public a few years ago:

Ten Days That Shook the World. Notice the one-syllable effect.

Why Johnny Can't Read. This could be adapted for Christian use: an article could be entitled, "Why V.B.S. Is Dying." Such shock technique should be used sparingly, but it should be used.

I Was a Teen-age Werewolf. This man combined two popular concepts, youth and horror, to make a fortune. Titles are important.

Finally, a couple of choice and original words at the end of your article will provide a fillip or a snap that will be just what you need to get your piece off dismal hill and onto the highway of hope. It could be an apt quote in the closing sentence from Winston Churchill or Omar Bradley or Josh Billings or Billy Graham or Barry Goldwater or Martin Luther King or Paul of Tarsus. Even one word might bring it off. Don't drift off into a "something ought to be done" line or a pointless "recap" of what you have already said. Use the last sentence to give the impact of a springboard, to start the reader thinking on his own.

Now go back to that particular article you have drafted and are anxious about. Do a little dreaming. Imagine you are trying to catch the attention of an editor who is sitting in a chair, being pressed on all sides by people who want him to read what they have in their hands. You must attract his attention. What will you do? You realize that you haven't stated it as forcefully as you might, so you take it back and rewrite it, making it more urgent. You think of little ways to catch his attention. You cater to his prejudices. You try to think his thoughts—you anticipate his needs—for somehow you have to get that paper into his hand. By now you have lost your natural reticence; you have become quite bold; you are willing to try any literary device that will work.

So you push your piece of writing at the man, and it has cockleburrs sticking all over it, and what happens? He reads it. Congratulations! You have just sold a story to an editor who did not have the least intention, when he picked up your manuscript, of spending more than 20 seconds on it. And you did it with words that screamed like fire engines and bounced like golf balls and went rat-tat-tat like woodpeckers. But when you talked about God, it was as the voice of many waters.

You see, you *can* put words together. You *can* become a voice of God in this generation. Who made the greatest impact in the twentieth century for Christ in the English language? Was it a preacher? No. It was an odd little man who sat in a stark study in Magdalen College in Cambridge, England, and his name was C. S. Lewis. This man, who lived a life that had a lot lacking in it, said more, did more, influenced more people high and low around the world than any preacher.

I interviewed him in 1963 just before he had

his heart attack, and he told me of the letters that would come to him from everywhere. He would answer each of them in his crowded handwriting. He never had a secretary, never had a typewriter, never had any of the things that we think are so important for writing. Yet C. S. Lewis made a tremendous impression for Jesus Christ. Why? Because he could use words.

7

THE LIGHT TOUCH

The light touch is an approach to Christian literature which seeks to make it readable. It moves on the premise that unless prose is interesting it is not worth perusing and therefore not worth writing. One secret of the light touch is that it brings out the incongruities in a situation. I believe that the incongruities of existence can be used for a double purpose: to evoke a bit of humor and to lead the reader on to faith. Both humor and faith deal with life's paradoxes. Laughter and trust are the ways in which we Christians reconcile ourselves to the great irreconcilable mysteries. Laughter tells us that it is a crazy, ridiculous, preposterous world, and that we had better learn to laugh or we shall find it impossible to live in it. Trust places those mysteries ultimately in the hands of a sovereign God.

The light touch which I am proposing to you is an English approach, by and large. One finds something similar in the French writers—Voltaire, de Maupassant, Anatole France, Sartre—but it always has a bitter edge. It is not so characteristic of German writing, which leans toward the heavy side. Slavic literature knows nothing of it, from Tolstoy to Gorky to Pasternak. Americans engage in a great deal of writing in the light vein, but our humor tends to become too contrived. Like Art Buchwald, we set out to do a funny piece. Buchwald's pieces can be very funny, but I am not speaking of funny pieces. I am speaking of a spirit that informs the whole, even much of the strong writing. I would say the late Halford Luccock is one of the better examples of the light American touch. Like G. K. Chesterton, R. H. Tawney, George Bernard Shaw, Charles Williams, and C. S. Lewis, he writes jocularly but with restraint. More recently Bob Friedman has written a gem, *What's a Nice Jewish Boy Like You Doing in the First Baptist Church?*

If you can master this touch, I am confident that it will speed you on your way, and that it will help market your articles quickly.

That is not all it will do! My wife wrote an article for the British Christian weekly, *The Life of Faith*. She described how she went into an antique shop and looked over an attractive jug, but resisted the temptation to buy it. Then she began witnessing to the proprietress, asking her if she had been to Earls Court to the Crusade, which Billy Graham was holding there at that time. The lady had not. My wife asked if she would like some tickets. The lady would be delighted. My wife gave her the tickets, said good-bye and left. But when she wrote the story my wife put it this way: " 'Good-bye,' I said, eyeing the jug for the last time."

You would not believe it, but when the article appeared, a lady subscriber read it, telephoned my wife, said what a pity she did not buy the jug, bought a whole suitcase full of antiques to give to the wives of members of the Billy Graham team, and then made a contribution to the Crusade!

What did the addition of those words do? It revealed the author as a human being, tempted in all points like the rest of us. This is the light touch. If you exhibit it in your writing, instead of the proud, holier-than-thou attitude or the listen-to-teacher maxims that pervade most of our religious literature, editors will be surprised and amazed. They may go into shock. Your writing will be no less earnest for being honest, but it will be more acceptable. Your writing will be more suggestive and less exhaustive. People will decide that they like the way you put things, and once they have decided that, you have a style. You are on your way.

Now, what are the qualities and characteristics of the light touch? *First, it betrays a healthy digestion.* If a man can see the whimsical side of life, we do not assume that he has no troubles; we feel that he has managed to rise above them. The writer who can do this can keep bile and dyspepsia from coming out on paper, no matter what his subject matter. And the reader unconsciously thinks, "The world has not got this fellow down. How come? Maybe I can learn something from him."

Second, the light touch has personal objectivity. The classic subject, of course, is a person's own inconsistencies and foibles. This can be overdone; we can exploit ourselves until people are sick of reading about us. But true personal objectivity is not self-obsession. It is simply a matter of refusing to take ourselves too seriously, even in Christian writing. Usually when a Christian writes, his subject matter is serious. He is talking about his Lord. The treasure is amethyst and sapphire and onyx, but remember that the vessel is earthen; that is to say, it is made of clay and mud.

I do not mean, as some modern theologians seem to imply, that the Christian should forget about holiness and set out to become more worldly than the world. There is nothing more pitiful than a Christian trying to "identify" with the world by imitating it. It certainly does not impress the man in the street. But the greatest saints were nothing but honest men and women with faith. They were great partly because they were willing to admit their humanity.

Third, the light touch is a writing tool. It can be used as a device or technique to make a point. Suppose you wish to interest your reader in a serious discussion of a fairly heavy subject—the need, let us say, for a new kind of Sunday school curriculum. To read a ponderous piece of literature requires effort. People are increasingly reluctant to put forth the effort. A light touch will carry the reader into a discussion without strain; he will find your opening paragraph rather engaging, and he will go along with you to see if there are any more like it. If you have further touches along the way—and you should, as any successful lecturer will tell you—then the curse of tedium will be taken off your piece, and people will decide that not only do you have something to say, as a Christian should, but you say it well.

Fourth, the light touch is Scripturally warranted. The man to whom the Bible is a closed book thinks of it as a series of thou-shalt-nots and list of begats and a collection of dire threatenings. I do not have to spend time explaining to you that this is not so. In fact, the light touch can be found in many parts of the Bible: in Genesis, in the books of Samuel and Kings, in the Psalms and Proverbs, in Jonah, and of course in the Gospels, particularly in the stories and parables of Jesus. I suggest that in your own Bible reading, you mark such passages with a colored pencil.

Now it is time to ask how one goes about learning to acquire and use this tool. So many of us in our private conversations are full of little dashes of humor, but when we sit down at the typewriter, we freeze. We say we can't think of a thing. The truth is, we think we are on display, so we try to put our best foot forward. That is another way of describing an ego trip. I would suggest that we perhaps ought to put our worst foot forward. It belongs to us too. But let's say just what we mean:

1. Exploit every bit of humor that there is in a situation. Any situation. You were on your way home from downtown, the buses were on strike, you waited for a taxi, it started to rain, you had just come from the beauty parlor, the umbrella

wouldn't work, your clothes began to shrink—give it everything you have.

2. Let your natural sense of drama take over. Tell it as you would over the telephone, or to a friend over a cup of coffee. Build up the suspense. If you have to rearrange the facts in order to make it a first-class story, then put it in third person and go to it.

3. Combine opposites. This is an effective method of producing a chuckle when it is properly done. And a chuckle means you have readers! I remember hearing a cowboy singing on the radio. He twanged away about all his tragic experiences: his horse stepped into a badger hole, someone set fire to the bunkhouse, his sweetheart deserted him, the drouth ruined the range, the herd of cattle died, the foreman let him go, and then he added, "Now I'm getting dandruff." When World War II broke out a friend of mine in Alaska said, "Pete writes from Idaho and says he's so discouraged by world conditions that he's not even going to cut his lawn." Call it the law of lessened effect, or a combination of opposites.

4. Couch what you say in descriptive language. The light touch depends a good deal on forsaking the old clichés and the drab adjectives and tire-

some adverbs that we use over and over again in our writing. This kind of thing comes by practice. It calls for a daily stint. Look around you. There is a great deal of comical material in connection with the stories others can tell you. Or take church. Toy with this subject for a moment: "How our house gets ready for church." Describe how you lay in bed Sunday morning and planned it all out, just how things would go, and then you got up and—well, it just didn't work out that way. The first thing that happened was—and you take it from there. Make it vivid, even flamboyant. If you need any encouragement, read the Gospels. Our Lord used extremely colorful language: "whited sepulchres," "gnashing of teeth," "that fox."

Now, the first draft of your writing will hardly amount to more than wild notes and jottings, put down hurriedly, perhaps even in suppressed excitement and laughter. Don't worry about style, about grammar, about anything. Just get it down. Let it bubble over. That will provide the raw material that you can build on later. The second draft will show the first signs of something taking shape, and will include a lot of embellishment of what you wrote first. Then the third draft gets down to something that you are seriously considering submitting to an editor. At this point I believe it is ready to be looked over by someone else with a critical eye.

Christians are, as I have suggested, supremely qualified to write in the vein of lightness. After all, it is a matter of vast relief to know that our burden of sin has been lifted, that we are forgiven, that our salvation is sure. It is enough to make anyone lighthearted. The world as we know it becomes increasingly complex; ours is not a very pleasant century, and many men have reacted to it by becoming bitter realists who are unwilling to take anything on faith. Romance, idealism, nobility—these are forgotten words. Today's literary craftsmen are angry young men and women. Their products are soiled with filth, brutality, desperation, and unbelief.

It is possible that the only light and pleasantly readable literature of the '70s will come from the typewriters of believers who face the future with confidence no matter what the human prospect. It is possible that we shall become the people who hold the literary world together. The challenge is ours.

8

THE STRONG TOUCH

What is the strong touch? I can think of no better description than the one contained in Matthew's Gospel: "He spoke as one having authority." The strong touch is the touch of the master, the mark of authenticity, the touch of an author who, while he is not infallible, knows what he is talking about, and who is acquainted with the divine element of truth behind his subject.

The strong touch is the touch of a strong person, and you can be that person.

Let us start by saying that the surest way to bring that touch to your writing is to plant in it liberally the good seed of the gospel. We have nothing else to compare with Jesus, nothing else in our quiver as powerful and significant. Our copy can be dead—just a lot of words strung one after another, cold and lifeless. Then we begin to move into what the poet Masefield called "the burning cataracts of Christ," and our typewriters begin to hum and purr.

So much average Christian writing never quite gets around to the law and the gospel. It buzzes about the outside petals but never crawls into the flower. It never tells us that the world is lost without God; that ours is a planet in revolt; that man was created in the image of God, but rebelled, and stands alienated today from God and man and corrupted by sin. Then the good news: that God has reconciled the world to himself through the life, death, and resurrection of Jesus Christ. Through him we are reunited with God and with one another, and set free from the bondage of sin and death.

You and I don't have to go into our favorite three points or four points or fourteen points of the faith every time we write a devotional; leave that to the theologians. It is an unfortunate fact that theological writers (at least the modern variety) do not win many of their readers to Christ. But novelists like Charles Williams can, and do. Dramatists like Dorothy Sayers can, and do. Poets like John Donne can, and do. Theology is important, but for a working writer what is vital is not his acquaintance with all the fine points of dogma; rather it is his ability to take a basic, elementary, solid grasp of gospel truth and make use of it in his writing. It has to be acceptable, of course; but that does not mean it cannot be aggressive.

I once read a book by one of those fellow-travelers who flirt with the edges of the gospel. The writer was saying, "You can be the person you like, if you dare." He was tossing in bits of psychology and group-think and summer camp inspiration; but it was weak tea. It had no New Testament stinger in it, no doctrine of sin. It lacked the strong touch of a supernatural God wrestling with men who need to be saved from hell.

When I suggest that you do not need a three-year course in systematic theology, I am not implying that the strong touch is a mark of ignorance. The gospel of Jesus Christ has a way of imparting wisdom even to those who are lacking in erudition. I think of a lay preacher like Billy Bray, the Cornish miner; or Pecos Higgins, the Arizona cowboy poet. I would pit these men in debate against an existentialist philosopher any time. The Holy Spirit has given gifts to many a humble believer that some of the greatest intellectuals yearn to have.

Mahalia Jackson's jingle shows us what can happen:

> See that there young preacher?
> He's fresh out of school,
> he don't know my Jesus,
> he's an educated fool.

The gospel of Jesus Christ can make writing interesting and it can make it strong. There will always be a concurrent need for literary artistry, for timing, for suspense, for descriptive setting, for characterization, for a dexterous use of words. But in the end it is the glad word of salvation that carries the knockout blow.

You can work it into a golf story. You can splice it into a murder mystery. You can use it to interpret a historical study. You can call on it to suffuse a poem with inspiration. You can employ it in one way or another in a devotional diary, a Christmas play, a biography, a testimony, a church article. Wedge it in! Remember that the word "preach" is related to the Greek word "euangelio." And that means "to proclaim the glad tidings." As Christian writers that is what we are called to do, whatever the form our writing takes. For we are unashamedly propagandists, out to win the world for Christ, not through a distortion of the truth but through the proclamation of the truth. For us to write, therefore, is to preach, to announce the glad tidings.

Well, then, do we have to insert John 3 or Romans 7 or Ephesians 2 every time we slip a fresh sheet into the typewriter? By no means. Let's hope we can be a little more ingenious than that. But somewhere along the way our faith has to shine through. Emil Brunner says of us ordinary Christians that there is something which "from love and in love we are to do to our neighbor in accordance with the will of the Creator and the Redeemer." He adds, "In cooperation we are to do what everyone does, and we are also to act differently from others." How? "At the right time and place," says Dr. Brunner, "the ordinary Christian will say something amazing, something which does not simply belong to the subject in hand, something unexpected, about God and eternal things, something which, just because it is said at an unusual time and in an unusual way, will have more demonstrative, attractive, and awakening power than the majority of sermons."

That is our challenge as Christian writers. I am assuming of course that you are in favor of the gospel. Many of our fellow-writers are not. If they go into the subject of "religion," it is to describe their revolt against the Christianity of their youth, their loathing of the church's discipline, their disillusionment with its so-called professors. So many contemporary authors use their books as a catharsis to explain and justify their flight from God. We on the other hand write to establish faith in God and in his gospel.

As Christian journalists we have a responsibility to tell the whole truth, the good as well as the bad. Imagine the Psalmist spending all his time complaining that the temple was too cold, and the incense was too thick, and the marble slabs were too hard on his knees! He would never have had time or energy to write the 100th Psalm, or the 139th, or the 150th. Suppose Luke had spent his time reporting the things Paul "failed to touch on" in his sermons in Asia Minor. I doubt if we would be reading the Book of Acts for devotions today.

Here are a few practical ways in which you can make the strong touch the hallmark of your own writing product. First, *tackle the great issues.* I know a writer who has published a good many casual pieces—good, mind you, but she would be categorized as a middleweight. Then one day she wrote on assignment a study of Dante to commemorate the 700th anniversary of his birth. I would say that Dante was a magnificent subject.

The great issues should be our meat and drink. Consider the subject of true love. We need to keep alive the flame of love in the literature of the next ten years. The whole concept is disappearing from culture and art forms. What is true love? Don't ask Freud. Don't ask Bertrand Russell. Don't ask Ian Fleming. Don't ask Jacqueline Susann. You are the one to be asked, and you are the one to give the answer.

Consider the subject of hope. If you cannot get hope into your writing, then you might as well trade in your typewriter for a color TV set. You must give us hope. We need you to tell us that Christianity works; that it issues in victorious, fruitful Christian living, no matter what the problem, no matter how desperate the situation; and that after death things get better yet.

Second, *get hold of something believable.* Once and for all, let's get our Christian writing out of the nineteenth century. Other people can hold back the times, but you cannot afford to. Your place is out front, beckoning. The old landmarks that Jeremiah warned us to observe, the old paths that he told us to walk in, they are out in front, too. God does not change; he is the eternal contemporary.

One radiant testimony by a born-again believer will torpedo all the arguments about the death of God and leave the radical theologian speechless. What can he say in reply? "One thing I know—

that whereas I was blind, now I see"—how do you answer that?

Get this kind of believability into your writing. Don't write about your mother's faith, write about your daughter's faith. We can't remember what your mother had to face, but we have an idea as to what your daughter is going through. Your mother probably may have tried to find some answer to *Main Street,* but your daughter is faced with *Sex and the Single Girl* and worse. Make it believable for today.

Third, your writing will be more likely to carry a strong touch if you *major in clarity.* Confused writing is the hallmark of our day. Ernst Kirschten, editorial writer for the St. Louis *Post-Dispatch,* says, "Write not that you may be understood, but that you cannot be misunderstood." I do not imply that one's whole thesis has to be set forth in the opening paragraphs. Let it develop naturally, but make it clear that you know what you are writing about. If two sides of a subject are called for, present them lucidly and honestly, so that the issues are clear and the reader can make up his mind. Two other thoughts under this heading: one, an arresting statement at the beginning will show us that you do know your field and will command attention. Second, unless you are making an issue of it, it is better to keep uncertainty out of your pages.

Fourth, *avoid the commonplace.* An editor once told me that he deliberately used second-quality material on the back page of his paper, and paid half the usual rate for it. I think this is a parable of what is wrong with Christian literature. We are deluged with second-rate stuff. There is absolutely no excuse for it. We have the grandest theme in the world, one that has produced the psalms, the poetry of Milton, the sermons of Spurgeon. We do not intend just to jack up the level of fillers and youth-club testimonials. We are pointing you right to the top.

Fifth, *follow the natural lines of your interest* and stick to them. If it be children's writing, work at it. Let that be your forte, your vocation. Develop it. Grow in it. Exactly the same could be said for writing of Sunday school curriculum, or story papers, or interviews, or social problem articles, or biographies, or poetry, or drama, or whatever the field. Versatility is good, but too much versatility can keep the strong touch out of your writing. It took me years to learn that I will never write short stories, or novels, or plays, or books of theology. I have struggled to learn something of these fields, but it would take another lifetime or two to master them. Meanwhile, I have learned to be a journalist. That is what I am, and I love it. On occasion I can pour some pretty thick maple syrup over my journalistic hot cakes.

Specialization does not really restrict the writer, any more than a study of the Gospel of John restricts the searcher after truth. You master your field, then you wake up one day to realize that some of the principles you have learned apply to other fields as well. But you learned your apprenticeship in this one groove.

Finally, I would say that strength can be added to your writing by *a judicious use of documentation.* We should have the standard reference books at our elbow. A good bibliography is always appreciated. We need to see that our statistics are accurate and our sources are reliable.

I thank God for what has been written about the gospel and what will be written. If, in the months ahead, people begin talking about a new "voice" from some corner of the Christian world, the chances are it will not be a "voice" at all. It will be the clacking of a typewriter as some evangelical sits down to share the Good News of Jesus Christ and his saving power. And with the help of the printers and binders and publishers and salesmen and bookstore owners, that Good News will go out to bless men and women everywhere, just as the letters of Paul gave courage and hope to the Christians of two thousand years ago, and have done so ever since, to the praise and glory of Jesus' name.

9

TO MARKET TO MARKET

I have said it scores of times in writing schools and I will repeat it here: if we have the motivation, the discipline, the tools, and the contacts, we can write and we will be published.

In this chapter we shall be considering only contacts. How do we make them? Let's begin on a level familiar to all of us: Our church puts out a bulletin each Sunday, and much of the space is wasted. If we write a little piece, perhaps a poem, of an inspirational or evangelistic nature, and give it to the minister, he will likely use it. In a couple of weeks we give him another piece with our name on it.

Why is it important that we use our name? It has nothing to do with ego-tripping; it is a professional matter. When we build our names as authors for the glory of God, we establish ourselves as writers whom people will want to read.

From the church bulletin we move up to the state denominational paper or perhaps to the local newspaper. If our story is worth it, we can make a stab at one of the national religious magazines. But "stab" is not an accurate word, for the writer should arrange his movements so he can pay a personal visit to the editor in his habitat. He should become acquainted with the publishing house, should study its publications, its catalog, and familiarize himself with the kind of Christian writing that the house is interested in publishing.

Let me share with you a particular problem faced by book editors. Each season they have a book list to prepare, and they want it to be a winner. In a highly competitive field, the list must be balanced; it must carry some outstanding names, some staple items, some exciting new offerings. That means the aggressive book editor is looking for a "discovery," for a new name that will prove to be a phenomenon in the publishing world. If he finds a book that will arrest people's attention, his list is made.

That is your book! Many young authors do not realize that while they are looking for markets, the publishers are looking for them. Here is Mrs. Farmer Brown living on the south 40 in Hudson, South Dakota. She is banging away at her typewriter on the kitchen table, producing something, but she doesn't know where to send it. And here is Editor Jones sitting in his office in New York or Chicago or Grand Rapids or Minneapolis, scratching his head and saying, "Wouldn't it be great if we could get something about the gospel from a down-to-earth farmer's wife?"

Inexperienced writers often fail to take a sensible approach to the editor or publisher. They put him on a pedestal, or they fancy him a forbidding person in a skyscraper on the eastern seaboard. They need to see the editor as one who is constantly looking for fresh writing talent, hoping that the next writer he meets will fill his need.

I have found that editors are looking for people who are aware of the times in which they live and who consistently write in the modern vein. The editors want material that is alive, that pulses with a feeling that "you know where you are." They want Christ in the market place. They want material that appeals to the young market, that reflects a zestful frame of mind, that avoids clichés, and that takes the reader right into the presence of the Lord.

Now we come to the book itself: what will it

say? What is the author's rationale, his reason for bringing a book into existence? Is the manuscript just an extension of his personal ego? If it is, I can guarantee that no publisher of integrity will be interested in it. The basic premise of a book worth publishing can be stated in one sentence. Even before the author sits down to draw up a rough outline, a thought seed should be sprouting in his mind.

Once the writer is able to state simply and clearly his idea for a book, he ought to be able to approach the subject from different perspectives. That is to say, he should be able to develop categories and components. After some study, being careful to avoid duplicating what has already been written in the field, the author can work out a table of contents that contains the outline of his book. He then should prepare a sample chapter, or even a few pages, and start making contacts.

Don't write the book and then go looking for a publisher. A new writer, particularly, should be in close contact with an editor who believes in him and can give him guidance. The editor knows the market; he knows the readership; and he knows what will sell. He must be listened to. I once took a table of contents and a few sample pages of a proposed book to an editor and sat in his office while he went through the copy. Within 15 minutes the deal was closed. However, I did not consult him during the writing of the book. The result was that I had to do it over again—a process that took seven months. Eventually it appeared and was successful, but I learned something. On the rewrite I submitted it two chapters at a time and begged for counsel.

Now let's assume that you are acquainted with an editor. I suggest you impose on him! For an editor to go to lunch with an author is standard operating procedure; it happens every day. Has it happened to you? I remember with amusement a writer who attended one of our schools in Britain, and then wrote a jingle that went:

> I write, rewrite, and write again
> I do my best, but here's the crunch:
> How can I afford to take
> Fifty editors out to lunch?

We need not "take out" 50 editors; we want only the editor in whom we are interested and in whose periodical we would like to be published. In a social situation presumably we will make some headway with him. If he doesn't know us as a person already, he will from this point on. No longer are we a faceless, unsolicited author.

We may be on our way to becoming one of the house writers.

Once we are published by our editor, it is not unlikely that he will call on us again, especially if he considers us his friend. Quite possibly if a story is breaking in our part of the world, he will ask us to cover it for him.

The *Writer's Market* and other sources are valuable in helping us to canvass the field in which we are writing. We should know the names of all the magazines in our immediate circle of interest and the names of their editors. Let us suppose you are interested in writing for a denominational woman's magazine. You should know the names of the magazines published by the Baptists, Lutherans, Methodists, Pentecostals, and others. You should know also what standard religious magazines regularly carry articles slanted toward women. And you ought to know who their editors are.

Authors can become acquainted with editors in many different ways. They can meet them at writers' schools and clinics. They can follow up routine query letters, as I have suggested, with personal visits to the office. I have found, both as a writer and an editor, that a very good way to establish this dialog is by the long-distance telephone. I once asked a major New York editor about this and he said, "Yes, every day I talk to about 20 authors by long-distance telephone."

I am not suggesting that the query letter be bypassed; it is still highly desirable. But in view of the editor's time problem, with trips that take him away from the office, I find the telephone most convenient. Knowing our own magazine's needs for the coming issues, I can give a quick response to a verbal query from an author.

Furthermore, as a Christian, I never want to leave an author with a blunt negative. I try to give him something else to think about. If he lives in an interesting part of the country, I may suggest a story that is developing in his area. But a wise editor will always remind such a writer that he has not commissioned the story, that everything depends on the way the copy reads when it actually arrives in the editorial office.

In the case of a book, the publisher may want to commission a professional free-lance writer to cover a major story—let's say in Bangladesh—and may advance him expenses to enable him to write it. I have known such writers to spend as much as $20,000 before the manuscript is finally delivered to the editor.

One of the best approaches to a magazine editor is by way of the calendar. The editor is usually quite calendar-conscious. He can never find enough good material on Christmas and Easter. But if he publishes a monthly magazine, he is also open to suggestions for timely articles on other important dates: Pentecost Sunday (May or June); Reformation Sunday (October); the Fourth of July; Labor Day or Back-to-School (September); Thanksgiving (November, or October in Canada); the beginning of Lent; and various other dates in the church year. He is also conscious of centenary observances, and in the 1970s we are awash with them.

Remember that the editor is only a front for the market. The real audience we want to reach is in the homes where the magazine is delivered or the book is read. The editor thinks he knows his readership; he is familiar with its reading tastes. When he scans our material, it is with that audience in view. Will this article evoke a favorable response? Will this book sell? He cannot afford too many wrong guesses. Walk a few moments in the editor's moccasins and it may do something to your writing. And when you talk with him, may I make a further suggestion? Ask him about his work, his aims and goals. See if there isn't some way that you can help him to reach those goals. Surprise him by your knowledge of his work.

Finally, remember that the editor is not going

around with his pockets filled with rejection slips. Would you like to know what is really in those pockets? Contracts! I repeat, he is looking for people just like you and as soon as he is convinced that you have what he wants, he will sign you up.

10

THE WAY OF A MANUSCRIPT

Loving hands lift the final draft of the manuscript from the typewriter. A last breathless reading ensues, punctuated by internal squeals of satisfaction; then those same hands place the precious pages into an envelope together with a second envelope, stamped and self-addressed. With high hopes the whole thing is sealed and committed to the capricious mercies of the postal service, en route to the editor of a magazine or a publisher of books.

So what happens?

Anything can happen—but it is not likely to. Seventy years ago Jack London wrote *The Call of the Wild* and mailed it to the *Saturday Evening Post*. In the return mail he received a check for one thousand dollars. What's wrong with that story is that we cannot relate to it. Jack London was a genius. We are not.

Yet for us who are mere mortals of terrestrial design and orbit, a clear distinction can be drawn between the amateur and the professional. The pro usually (not always) knows when he sends out his manuscript that it stands a good chance of acceptance. He knows his market and he knows his editor. He knows when to send it and how much to expect from it. Most important, he knows what kind of material to put into his piece, and how to slant it.

The amateur, not knowing much about the market, has not given it much thought. He was concentrating on self-expression! His chances when he sends out a manuscript are something less than excellent.

If there is one person in the world with whom I empathize today, it is the lonely, isolated author who wants to write, has the story to share, believes in his qualifications, works hard at his typewriter, and gets nowhere. I know all about it and believe me, it doesn't have to be that way. Let me repeat: if a writer has the motivation, the discipline, the tools and the contacts, he can and he will be published. Of course if he has imagination—or what other people call "talent"—it helps, but I won't insist on it. I'm not sure that Abraham Lincoln had talent, but he had a dictionary and the back of an envelope, and he had something to say.

In the early years of *Decision* magazine, as we sifted through our fast-growing pile of unsolicited manuscripts, it became apparent to our staff that something was wrong either with the contributors or with us. No one was hitting our target. Most writers couldn't even find our shooting range.

In 1963, to remedy the situation, we launched our first three-day School of Christian Writing at the Billy Graham headquarters in Minneapolis, Minnesota. It has been an annual event ever since, and enrollment has had to be restricted. Meanwhile other annual schools have followed the pattern in California, Oregon, Illinois, and Ontario, and similar schools have been held in 15 countries of Asia, South America, Africa, Europe, and the South Pacific.

Many of the articles we are currently using in *Decision* have come from writers we have met through the schools. Several thousand of them have taken the course, including ministers, executives, teachers, journalists, pilots, nuns, professional people, farm wives, and teen-agers. We cultivate these writers; we challenge them and publish them whenever possible. If they sell to another magazine, or are successful in placing a book, it is a matter of genuine pride with us, for we look upon them as members of our family.

The way of a manuscript at *Decision* is probably not greatly different from its reception at other publication offices. If I were to detail the procedure we follow in handling a potential article, it would probably go like this:

1. *Initial query*. We receive a letter from someone who has an article or an idea for an article. A reply goes to the author indicating the extent of our interest. We suggest a 2000-word length, for we want a full discussion on the subject, though the edited article may be half that length.

2. *Arrival of manuscript*. It is glanced at by the editor and given a routing slip. For the next two to three weeks it is read by six different editors in succession. Each appends a comment and votes to accept or reject.

3. *Editorial decision*. If the manuscript is unsuitable, the editor or one of the editorial associates returns it with a personal letter. Sometimes the editors' comments are enclosed. If the manuscript is considered favorable, it is placed on the editor's desk. He studies it and then may give it

to the typist, who will make a rough copy to measure length.

4. *Revision.* This may be done by returning the manuscript to the author with suggestions. The letter may be written by the editor, incorporating the suggestions of the other editors. It may be handled in an editorial conference with the author, in person or by telephone.

5. *Retyping.* This prepares a working copy. It is given a different kind of routing slip and circulated to the editors for the crucial editing. The title and probable date of publication are now assigned it by the editor.

6. *Editorial conference.* If the manuscript is favorably regarded by the staff, the final detailed work of editing can be disposed of quickly in a conference between the copy editor and the editor. If problems persist, photostats may be made and the article will be gone over sentence by sentence in full editorial conference. We now consider the illustration, photographic or otherwise. We send a biographical form to the author.

7. *Final typing.* Perhaps only a page or two needs retyping at this stage. The article is marked for the typesetter, recorded, and sent out for type-

setting. A copy is sent to the author to secure his approval in its final typed form.

8. *Published form.* A copy of the article as it appears in print in *Decision* is airmailed to the author.

Why do we spend so much time and take such pains editing the manuscript? Because we believe God requires quality workmanship. He expected it in the building of the temple, and he expects it in the building of a magazine. We also are concerned to protect the author and to protect ourselves. Each statement of fact is checked by researchers to ascertain its accuracy. Quotations are traced to their source, if possible. We have a 6000-volume library that specializes in dictionaries and encyclopedias. If Thomas Carlyle made a certain statement, we don't want it attributed to John Wesley. If the Indonesians prefer to spell Djakarta with a D, we don't want to drop it; we have subscribers in Java.

The best suggestion I can give to anyone who wishes to be published in a magazine is, study the magazine carefully. See what the editor is attempting to do. By all means make contact with him if possible; take him to lunch; talk to him about his goals and purposes. If he edits a Christian magazine, talk with him about the Lord. I would encourage prospective writers to examine the balance in each issue of a magazine. There is nothing mysterious about it. In *Decision* we always attempt to carry a Billy Graham article, a team member's article, a woman's article, a youth article, a Bible teaching message, a testimony, a heritage article from the past, and something about evangelism or missions. Somewhere we tell how to find Christ.

Closely allied to our textual matter is the layout, which matches copy and illustrations. We will cross mountains and oceans to get the right photograph. If a writer can supply us with a good photograph to accompany his article, we are grateful; but often we prefer to take our own pictures. We attempt to present the material in the most up-to-date, attractive way we know. We are careful in choice of type, in the use of white space, and in the arrangement of the material on the page.

Finally, notice the care with which each article is prepared. Haphazard documentation has been the habit in the church for too long. We try to be as accurate as the *Journal of the American Medical Association*. Each statement of fact is researched. We are not afraid of footnotes, for we find that our readers appreciate our efforts to be thorough. When we make a mistake we make it several million times, and we don't care for that kind of advertising. On the other hand, when we come up with an exciting lead, when we catch the reader's interest with a photograph, when we exalt the Lord Jesus Christ by a good page treatment, and when letters come in telling of souls saved through the reading of *Decision,* our hearts are lifted up, and we give praise to the Lord of the alphabet.

11

RECYCLING YOUR ARTICLE

We Christian writers should be thinking all the time of ways and means to get more mileage out of our manuscripts. If it worked once, it should work again. For example, if you are writing a newspaper column, try to talk the newspaper into publishing a selection of your best columns in book form. If a devotional page, then collect them for a booklet. The same is true of cartoons, poems, and children's stories.

The Book of Psalms is a good illustration of recycling. Who knows what the original situation was in which those psalms were written? We are given a few hints, that is all. They, under the influence of the Holy Spirit, were collected and recycled, and have blessed the whole human race.

Sometimes an author's work is recycled after his death. That is happening today to C. S. Lewis. Somervell took six volumes of Toynbee and recycled them as one volume. I am having a wonderful time recycling some of the great writings of the past—Augustine, Bunyan, Patrick, Athanasius, Brother Lawrence, Teresa, Lady Julian, Thomas à Kempis, and many others.

But what I would really like to discuss is the recycling of the manuscript that has not yet been published. You wrote it, you sent it out, and it came back. Now what?

1. Make sure the manuscript is not still in the hands of an editor before you begin recycling. The obvious reason for that is that you may be embarrassed by selling the article twice. That has happened to people I know. They have sent the same article to two different publishers, have been accepted by both, and then have had to write one and say, "I'm sorry, you can't have it." This serves to blacklist the author in the eyes of the publisher. He won't sell anything there again for a while because they will never be sure. You find out about another publisher through the *Writer's Market* and you want to give him a try. Well, get the manuscript back first!

2. Keep a file of everything, in a filing cabinet,

under the title of the piece, alphabetically. Never, never send out a manuscript without keeping a copy.

3. Find out from the editor exactly why it was rejected. Perhaps there is something seriously wrong with the manuscript. If there is something wrong, I urge you to move heaven and earth to locate that bug.

The editor is the person who can help you, if he will. However, he has to be convinced that you don't have a hang-up; you don't have feelings of pride that will get in the way of your absorbing professional opinion regarding your product. If he thinks you will be embarrassed or miffed or put off by what he says, he won't say anything. Or, he'll say something bland like the wording of a rejection slip. If he really thinks you want to know, and you won't take offense, he will tell you what you want to know. He will be glad to, because he wants to help you and encourage you.

I think one of the hardest lessons any professional has to learn is to beg for criticism. It's fun to sit in a critique group and see one's friends take it on the chin. Can they handle it as well as dish it out? We say to them, "This is not really a solid piece of writing," and they take that and swallow it. But they still try to reach for a few crumbs. We all do. Well, I would say if you can adopt that attitude, you're going to be a writer.

4. Just rewrite it. Perhaps all this reject needed was a little more work and a little more polish. You sent it off before it was ready. Well, slip a piece of paper in the typewriter and try again. I remember a man saying once that as a minister he had often left a home without praying and later regretted it, but he had never left a home after praying and later regretted it. I can say that I have never rewritten an article another time and regretted it. I always was able to improve it even if it was just the punctuation, by running it through just once more.

If there is any doubt in your mind, take that nice clean manuscript that's come back with a rejection slip attached, sit down in your easy chair, and with your pencil in hand start to go through it. Read it again and then you'll say, "Well, I see that could have been changed—too many adjectives in that sentence"—or whatever it is. Then by the time you've read it again, you've got it penciled. Now it's time for retyping. I think a lot of our manuscript problems could be taken care of by just a little rewriting.

5. Salvage the best feature of the piece. Work it up by itself. If it be a poem, out of a long epic

poem, a few lines may be really good. Well, let's go with those lines and not worry about the epic.

There are four lines that I salvaged out of a poem by a lady from Sidney, New York. In the midst of all the rest of it, she had written this:

> Crumbled desires
> crushed pride
> bruised heart
> salvage for God.

I like that because it has the idea that God can take the broken pieces of life and put them back together and make something out of us. In other words, it has hope in it. So, I'm going to use that. But for the whole poem—it isn't suitable; it doesn't meet our needs. Sometimes three or four good lines can be lifted from a poem of thirty or forty lines!

This is also true about articles. Sometimes you may have a good illustration and work with it. It's like the oyster and the pearl. You build on it and wrap things around it, and pretty soon you've got an article. You send it in—and it's rejected! The editor might even say, "You had a good idea there." Well, the idea was the illustration, and that was really the best thing about the piece. Why not salvage the illustration? Why not lift that out and send that in? Every magazine has corners and little holes, because editors are very conscious of the fact that solid type on a page has low readability. If we can break it up with art work, white space, large type, or a poem, that will make people more interested in reading the message that's on that page. So we say, take the best feature of the piece that has been rejected and work it up by itself.

What is the best feature? You can ask your friends again, and they will quickly pinpoint it for you. It will be that which is most interesting to the average reader.

6. Try casting the piece in a totally different form. If it was a devotional, try working it up as a dialog, or make it a children's story, or make it a play. Add to it or shorten it or do something different with it.

Maybe that's not what it needs. If you have had a number of people who have taken a poor view of the piece, that's a pretty good indication that something has to be changed. It needs to be attacked from a different point of view. That leads me to the seventh point.

7. Forget the piece of writing you have done which has been rejected as such, but use the idea behind it as a stimulant to a fresh piece. Several editorials on which I have labored are sitting in

a file which is marked "Editorials," but they will never see the light of day. But I have taken an idea from them and have used it to make an entirely different editorial.

My associates are rather amused that I am tenacious enough not to give up this original idea, but they sec now that I couched it in different form, and they are willing to give it another try. They threw it out once; maybe this will go, and so they attack it afresh.

Writing from a completely different angle—perhaps moving it from third person to first person—or vice versa—will often help. The original thought that you had was sound, you understand, but it needed a different kind of execution.

8. Send it out again, but make sure you don't send it back to the same editor. You wouldn't believe it, but manuscripts have come back to us untouched, unchanged from the person whom we've already rejected, but who said, "I just can't believe that you would reject this manuscript, so I'm giving it to you again." Well, I can be just as stubborn.

I don't need to tell you that many, many books have been sent out again and again and have been rejected. Finally they have been accepted and have turned out to be literary events. The classic illustration is *The Living Bible* which Kenneth Taylor started when he was working for a publishing house. He sent it to one publisher, which rejected it. Taylor tried some other places, and finally he published it himself. You've heard about this sort of thing. I think it has passed the 19 million mark in sales. Don't let me encourage you to try being your own publisher, however; you're not Kenneth Taylor and neither am I.

Keep sending it out. If you believe in the manuscript and your friends believe in it, and they're not just trying to coddle you or make you feel good by stroking your fur, go ahead. Send it out again, and perhaps from different people you'll get different reactions as to how to improve it if they don't accept it.

9. Read the manuscript to your critique group, with the comments of the editor who rejected it. Don't ask for sympathy and don't try to justify yourself, or argue why you think it's good. You can explain what you meant, of course, but they may come back at you with, "Why didn't you say that?" Clarity of expression is one of our major goals. You know in your heart that maybe they're wrong. Sometimes our critics are wrong, of course. And we must never pay so much attention to our critics that we get discouraged, or

lose our creative urge. But on the other hand they are trying to help us. If they shoot holes in our boat, they'll hand us a bailing bucket. Remember that you are a pro, and pros don't cry. When you get these people to express themselves, write down their comments. Then you go back and you tackle the rewriting.

10. Don't pass up a chance to get your reject into print. That is to say, if you are rejected by Mr. A, you may hear about Mr. B whom you don't know, who may want material like yours. In your discussions with fellow writers, this kind of news is always bubbling to the surface. Don't pass up the chance to dig out what you have. Dust it off and send it in.

Another thought: If your published writings are to be collected in a paperback, why not sneak that reject in with the others? It was just as good. Same author. It just might make it, and then you will have it recycled.

11. Don't worry about what's in your file. A quarterback only completes a certain percentage of his passes. All of the great writers left behind cartons of unpublished manuscripts—Lewis, Wolfe, Hemingway, Kafka. Once in a while a publisher will release an "early book of Joyce Cary" or someone else, and it really doesn't have

much popular appeal. The author knew that it didn't measure up to his best work, so was quite content to leave it there in the file. It was a part of his development as a writer.

A lot of material that we write becomes superseded by something that somebody else has done. I wrote to a lady just the other day and said, "We can't use this piece. But look what it did for you. It gave you good practice in writing and it gave you valuable experience in interviewing. You're a better writer now for having done this." It may seem like sour grapes, but it's true that the writing you've done has helped to make you a better writer. Don't think it's wasted. I don't think that all those card parties I used to write up as a reporter for the Alaska *Daily Press* and the Hilo *Tribune Herald* were wasted. They were what we used to call "boiler plate"; crank it out, day after day, six days a week. But as a result, I became familiar with words. They became my tools. I can tackle a story now without hesitation, confident, knowing something will come out on paper, something that has a reasonable congruence to the event it describes. Writing every day gave me that confidence.

Your idea for that unsalable article may not have been sound. Don't become over-attached to it. Don't be obsessed by a determination to see it published.

People tell me, "I want to write a book about my dad."

I ask, "Why? As a filial tribute? I'm sure he's a good man, but have you considered the market?" Write to be published, and you will be published. Write for any other reason and you're in trouble.

12. Remember that your best writing is always yet to come. While endeavoring to recycle your old stuff, be sure that you are engaged in something new and fresh.

I ask people, "What are you working on now?" If they say, "I'm still trying to do something with that thing they keep sending back," I groan mentally. Keep looking for new ideas! The experience you have tomorrow may be the catalyst that will get you into print in a big way. God's mercies are new every morning, and so are our writing opportunities.